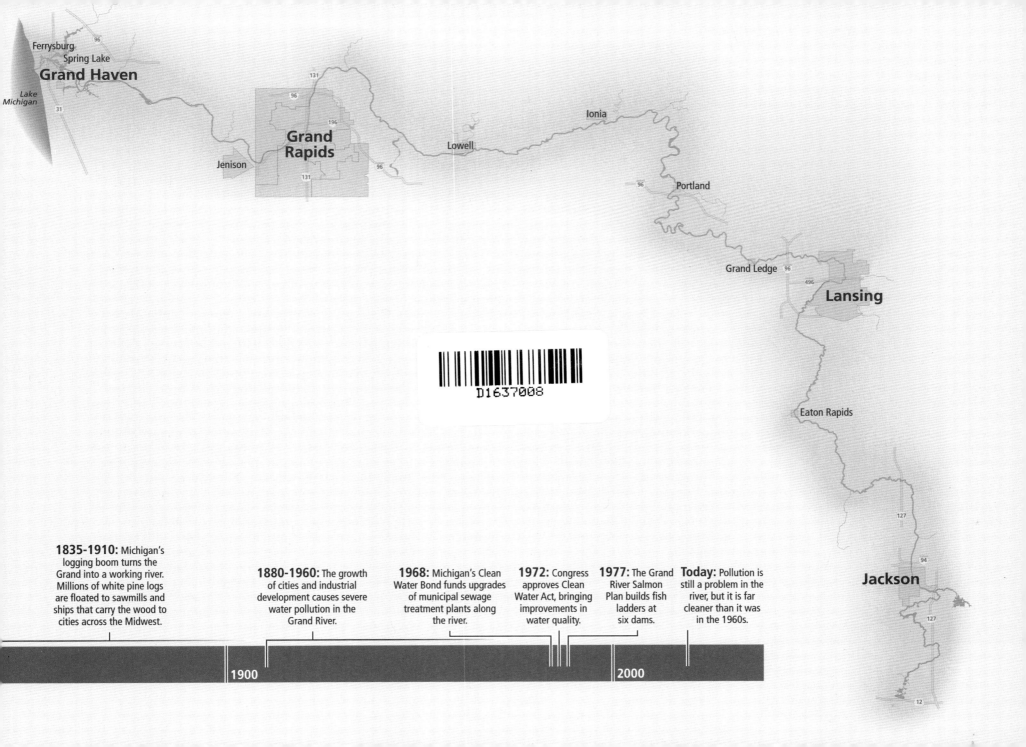

Ferrysburg
Spring Lake
Grand Haven

Lake Michigan

96

131

Grand Rapids

96

196

Jenison

131

Ionia

Lowell

Portland

96

Grand Ledge

496

Lansing

Eaton Rapids

D1637008

127

94

Jackson

127

12

1835-1910: Michigan's logging boom turns the Grand into a working river. Millions of white pine logs are floated to sawmills and ships that carry the wood to cities across the Midwest.

1880-1960: The growth of cities and industrial development causes severe water pollution in the Grand River.

1968: Michigan's Clean Water Bond funds upgrades of municipal sewage treatment plants along the river.

1972: Congress approves Clean Water Act, bringing improvements in water quality.

1977: The Grand River Salmon Plan builds fish ladders at six dams.

Today: Pollution is still a problem in the river, but it is far cleaner than it was in the 1960s.

1900

2000

OUR GRAND JOURNEY

Discovering the river we thought we knew

Published by

Danny R. Gaydou, Publisher

A depiction of a woman who may have traveled the Grand centuries ago.

Grand Rapids brings its own kind of life to the night.

ACKNOWLEDGMENTS

OUR GRAND JOURNEY
Project Staff

Editor - Paul Keep

Project Coordinator, The Grand Tour Series on the
Grand River/Book Editor - Peg West

Writers - Jeff Alexander, Howard Meyerson

Photo Editor/Layout - Chris Clark

Lead Photographer - Rex Larsen

Photographers - Katy Batdorff, Mark Copier, T.J. Hamilton,
Joel Hawksley, Marcia Huff, Paul L. Newby II, Cory Olsen,
Dave Weatherwax, Emily Zoladz

Photo Assistant - Chris Huntoon

Cover Design - Steve Young

Design - Paul Richmond

Marketing Director - Mary Oudsema

Marketing Project Manager - Debra Novak

Cover photo:
This aerial shot by Rex Larsen captures early morning
on the Grand, near Ionia.

Right: Kent Trails bridge in Grand Rapids.

CONTENTS _____

Between Liberty and Michigan Center.

FOREWORD

It's such a constant, we take it for granted.

Oh, we notice the Grand River. We glance at the river as we cross it. We bemoan when it breaches its banks. We boat on it. We watch the reflections of bridge lights dance on it, and as fish try to make their way against its swift current.

But how well do we really know the Grand River?

Over 17 days, The Press took readers on a discovery tour, and we re-introduced ourselves to this 262-mile river, the longest in the state. We followed the Grand River Expedition, held every 10 years to draw attention to the river's water quality. In the process learned more about this waterway that defines a region.

But this series was about more than learning. It really seemed to strike a chord with readers, who reveled in the magnificent photos from vantage points they likely will never know and in the stories about the people and communities along the river, as well as the waterway's many personalities.

The daily expedition diaries, especially, showcased how in a matter of hours, or in some cases less than that, the river changes drastically. Paddlers wove through a lovely Ingham County greenway in the morning only to reach the wide, busy urban waters of Lansing in the afternoon.

When Outdoors Editor Howard Meyerson, who paddled that stretch for The Press, called me at the end of the day, he pronounced the ride "intense."

I also recall Howard's account of going through the harsh industrial corridor of Grand Rapids, and then, minutes later, hitting a lovely pocket of peaceful paddling.

The river was narrow and log-choked. It was slow and smelly. Birds of prey soared overhead. In the cities, the drone of modern highways was the backdrop for those traveling in kayaks along the ancient highway. It was the playground for boaters and jet skiers, especially as it got closer to Lake Michigan.

I found myself a little smitten with this mercurial river.

Maybe that's because it was the first time I had truly contemplated it. I have lived in the river's vicinity my entire life, and spent meaningful chunks of time on two tributaries, the Rogue and the Red Cedar.

But I never really thought about how this river and its tributaries connect all of us until I read how expedition members christened during opening ceremonies a monument that bears an inscription about the headwaters. People took turns announcing the name of a Grand tributary, then poured water collected from that waterway onto the boulder, which the glaciers had moved from Canada to Jackson County. Some Lake Michigan water was also rightly included, to remind us where the Grand is headed.

The symbolism was humbling: They all contribute to the Grand, and the Grand contributes to all of us.

While that connection makes disparate cousins of such communities as Onondaga and Grand Rapids, it also spans generations. Perhaps you found yourself thinking about the Indians and early explorers to whom the waterway was vital to travel, and wondered what they must have thought of the grand ledges and other splendor. Perhaps you found yourself pondering how the river helped build the industry that became the backbone of our state and sustained our own families for decades.

Maybe you thought about the communities that came to be because of the river. Or are named because of it.

Or maybe you just flashed back to a favorite camping spot along the Grand as a kid.

There's a romantic notion to this waterway that starts as a stream and ends as a mighty river feeding beautiful Lake Michigan. Each day of the series the river unfolded before us, growing with each tributary, occasionally harnessed, always offering a new look.

Turns out there is so much more to know about this river than we glean in a glance while hurrying over the Sixth Street Bridge or gobbling lunch for a few minutes at a riverside park.

We hope you enjoy re-living the journey along the Grand with us in this book.

Peg West
Project coordinator for The Grand Tour series on the Grand River

AN INTRODUCTION TO THE GRAND RIVER

The Grand River's history is one of ruin and recovery.

It is a tale of 19th century loggers, booming cities and 20th century manufacturers using the Grand as a sewer until the 1970s, followed by a generation of community leaders, government officials and environmental activists working to revive the ailing river.

This 262-mile river refused to die, despite more than a century of vile pollution by sawmills, municipal sewage, metal plating firms, meat-packing plants, a tannery and other industries.

Experts say the Grand River is as healthy today as it has been at any time in the past 100 years.

Serious problems remain – including polluted storm water runoff, sewage overflows, wetland destruction and 14 dams in the main branch and another 218 dams in its tributaries that have divided the sprawling ecosystem into a series of smaller, ecologically dysfunctional streams.

Still, scientists who have studied the river said the Grand is an example of how effective regulations can restore troubled ecosystems.

Limits on industrial discharges and dramatic reductions in sewage overflows in the city of Grand Rapids have improved water quality and bolstered fish populations over the past four decades, said Scott Hanshue, a fisheries research biologist for the Michigan Department of Natural Resources and Environment.

Hanshue has spent several years studying the river as part of a comprehensive assessment for the state. His conclusion: The Grand's recovery has been remarkable but incomplete.

"We're not going to be able to restore the Grand River to its pre-settlement condition, but we can rehabilitate it," Hanshue said.

One of the biggest challenges facing the Grand may be shedding the lingering perception that it is a filthy waterway unfit for man or beast.

"There are a lot of misconceptions about the Grand River because it was used as a sewer for a long time," said Mike Smith, a Portland resident and renowned paddler who counts the Grand among his favorites.

There is no mistaking the river's impact on the region.

Its network of wetlands and marshes, lakes and bayous, gurgling streams and powerful rivers support a plethora of wildlife: 95 native fish species, 215 bird species and 50 species of mammals, according to state data.

And the Grand River watershed is, in a word, huge. It drains 5,572 square miles of landscape in southern Michigan and accounts for 13 percent of Lake Michigan's entire drainage basin.

The river springs to life in wetlands in northern Hillsdale County, about 12 miles south of Jackson. It winds through vast marshes, farms, remote wooded areas and within two blocks of the state capitol, past towering rock ledges, miles of undeveloped land and the state's second-largest city before sprawling into a delta near Grand Haven and emptying into Lake Michigan.

It evolves from a lazy stream in Jackson to a mighty river once it reaches Grand Rapids, with the help of several major tributaries – including the Red Cedar, Looking Glass, Maple, Flat, Thornapple and Rogue rivers.

The Grand was an aquatic highway that carried Native Americans – Chippewa Indians gave the river its first name: "Owashtanong," meaning far-flowing water – fur traders and loggers across southern Michigan. The river and its tributaries gave rise to dozens of communities, which used the river to power sawmills and grain mills, irrigate crops, and transport logs that built cities across the Midwest and fed Grand Rapids' furniture industry. Factories also used the river's water to cool machinery.

Before dams were built in 1849 to harness the river's power and accommodate large boats, the Grand sloped 18 feet in one mile, creating whitewater rapids in the heart of Grand Rapids.

The mid-1800s marked the beginning of prolonged abuse of the river. By 1880, growing communities, logging waste and the clear-cutting of Michigan's white pine forests had choked the river with sawdust, huge amounts of sediment from the barren landscape and all manner of human and industrial waste.

Hanshue said cities and industries continued to use the Grand and other rivers as sewers until 1972, when the federal Clean Water Act set limits on the amount of chemical and biological waste that could be discharged into surface waters.

The river has come a long way since the environmental dark ages of the 19th and early 20th centuries. In 1905, the Grand Rapids Evening Press predicted the Grand would be more of a sewer than a river by 2005.

Walker resident Bob Strek, who has fished the lower river for four decades, said he marvels at the Grand's resurgence every time he sees it.

"When I was a kid (in the 1950s) we didn't fish or swim in the river; my Dad wouldn't let us," Strek said. "Now it's a really good fishery. It makes me feel good to see the river recover."

The dam at Liberty Pond.

THE UPPER GRAND

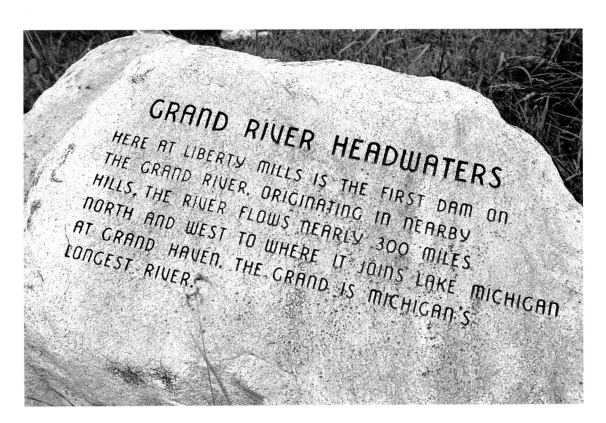

GRAND RIVER HEADWATERS

HERE AT LIBERTY MILLS IS THE FIRST DAM ON THE GRAND RIVER. ORIGINATING IN NEARBY HILLS, THE RIVER FLOWS NEARLY 300 MILES NORTH AND WEST TO WHERE IT JOINS LAKE MICHIGAN AT GRAND HAVEN. THE GRAND IS MICHIGAN'S LONGEST RIVER.

For something so grand, it starts out humbly.

The Grand River's upper reaches are often marshy and full of natural obstacles, so much so that expedition organizers could not launch at the headwaters in Liberty, opting instead to start upstream in Michigan Center.

That nascent character is evident even as the river goes through Jackson, its first major city. It is narrow here, just wide enough for kayaks in some places.

But then tributaries like the Portage River start making deposits, adding some heft.

And foretelling what is to come.

LIBERTY – It is hard to imagine the narrow stream behind the General Store here in the headwaters of the Grand River was once part of the "deepest and most important rivers in North America." That would have been 14,000 years ago, in the time of melting glaciers, according to Douglas author Kit Lane, who wrote, "The Grand," a book that traces the river's history.

Lane writes that the Grand was more than 100 feet deep in places. It was a scoured-out channel in the earth that drained off glacial melt water.

That isn't the river the 2010 Grand River expedition saw. But the river they came to know is certainly grand: At 262 miles it is the longest river in the state.

But it is also a mere approximation of its ancestral kin. Natural evolution and human footprints have made it very different.

"The biggest issues we face today are fragmentation due to the dams and road crossings," said Scott Hanshue, a Michigan Department of Natural Resources and Environment fish habitat biologist and author of a state management plan for the river.

There are six major dams on the mainstem of the river, he said, 232 in total on its various tributaries in the Grand River watershed. There are 8,000 road crossings too.

Those dams and culverts affect fish passage upstream. They raise water temperature and create sedimentation issues. Undersized culverts can become high-pressure water jets during storms. All of this has a role in determining which species thrive.

The fishery is spotty here. There are largemouth bass, bluegill and northern pike, but "it's a modest stream fishery," Hanshue said. "Most fishing takes place in the inland lakes until you get north of Jackson."

The upper river flows out of small spring-fed lakes and gathers volume as it travels north to Lansing before veering west.

The river is small and undistinguished as it meanders through communities like Liberty and Michigan Center, where some know it as the Grand; where others know it as the little outlet from Center Lake where you can sit and catch a bass.

"It's got a bigger name than it appears," said Rachel Matthews, an environmental quality analyst with the DNRE Jackson office. "It is just beginning in the Jackson area. People's contact with it in southern Jackson County is in the form of this lake or that lake. People see them as lakes, not the beginning of a river system."

The quaint stream at Liberty takes on quite a different appearance in the city of Jackson, a short drive by car and several hours downstream by canoe. In downtown Jackson it is confined to a half-mile concrete sluiceway built to handle sewage. The trough was eventually capped with concrete to reduce the odor and keep city residents from dumping their trash.

The cap was removed in 2001 after several children drowned in the canal. The tragedies are memorialized with crosses mounted on the fence beside the river there. They are a stark contrast to the beautification efforts that are under way by the city and its corporate neighbors. Consumers Energy, which has its headquarters across the street from the memorial, built a small scenic park with a bench along the canal.

Jackson, like other cities, has worked to separate its storm water sewer from its sanitary sewer. They were once combined and both would flow into the Grand River during big storm events. Storm runoff still goes there, but raw sewage doesn't, said Paul Rentschler, a water quality consultant in the Jackson area and staff ecologist for the Upper Grand River Watershed Alliance.

At least, it isn't supposed to be going there.

"There is still some aftermath from the old system," Rentschler said. "The communities are working on it."

The water quality focus has shifted over the years, according to Rentschler. The Clean Water Act helped get a handle on "point-source" pollution, like the discharges from industrial operations.

But development in the region is increasingly covering permeable soils with pavement. That, in turn, channels more storm water into the system. Those waters carry whatever they come in contact with on roofs and driveways and parking lots. And there are fewer acres of permeable soils to help filter out pollutants.

The Grand River flows from downtown Jackson into a residential area. It then passes through an industrial corridor before cutting through suburbs and into more wooded natural and rural areas.

Between Jackson and Rives Junction its volume increases. Additions from the Portage River add to its flow, making it wider and deeper. Additional creeks and streams add volume as it moves north.

The Grand then cuts through flood plain zones where trees fall and logjams build. It moves out through the countryside into farmland, big agricultural fields where row crops are grown, where agricultural runoff presents yet another challenge.

But the river is wider there, more wild in feel. The current picks up and the downed trees become just another challenge for area canoers and kayakers who enjoy paddling there.

North of Jackson, wildlife viewing, however, picks up, Hanshue said. Deer can be seen along the banks. A number of endangered or threatened species also are found there.

The common moorhen is a marsh dweller that can be found upriver, but not down. The American bittern, cerulean warbler, king rail and bald eagle are some of the other challenged species that live along the Grand.

Keen observers may find an endangered Blanding turtle or Eastern box turtle along the river, according to Hanshue. The Massasauga rattlesnake is also a river denizen. It is a species of "special concern" in Michigan and is protected by law.

Two Michigan Audubon Society bird sanctuaries are located nearby, both on tributaries of the Grand River. Audubon's Kate Palmer Sanctuary is on Sandstone Creek. Its Phyllis Haehnle Memorial Sanctuary - U.C.S., famous for its sandhill cranes, is on the Portage River, according to Matthews.

"Years ago you would bring people to Jackson County for the golfing. Now people want to bring them in for the bird watching," Matthews said. "There is a lot of nature and wildlife photography that happens here, though mostly on the Grand's tributaries."

This tour wasn't by paddle, but by foot.

To get a full appreciation of the river system, a group walked through the headwaters in Liberty, exploring a healthy prairie fen where the natural richness captivated some walkers.

Right: Brittany Ehman of Lansing tries to catch fish.

Far right: The cool clear waters fill the hands of Robert Miller of Holland, to his delight. "You get the impression you could scoop this up and drink it."

Walking through the headwaters.

Jim Seitz of Jackson glides under a highway bridge between Michigan Center and Jackson.

A great blue heron perches near a nest.

ROOKERY

It was like something out of Jurassic Park.

You could hear the great blue herons before you saw them, their screeches echoing through the treetops.

On a kayak trip through a narrow stretch of the Grand, 15 miles from the headwaters, with veteran local paddlers Kathy Kulchinski, Rick Berry and Kenny Price, Kulchinski remarked it was lucky to find the heron rookery. The swollen river that flooded the dark woods had spilled over a levee built many years ago by prison labor.

continued next page

Kenny Price of Jackson photographs great blue herons.

Through the dense treetop foliage we saw glimpses of dozens of sprawling nests with immature herons and adults. Occasionally a bird would launch from a branch, revealing its impressive wingspan. The sightings included a few great egrets.

"Few people have seen this" said Kulchinski as she put her camera down, and after an hour and a half of bird watching, led the group back downstream. "We were lucky today."

Above: An egret perches in a treetop.

Right: Looking for great blue heron nests.

A little oomph: Keanan France of Jackson thrusts his kayak over a dam near Michigan Center after briefly getting hung up on it.

Between Michigan Center and Jackson.

JACKSON

The river is narrow as it goes through Jackson, but not insignificant.

Its main feature is a half-mile concrete sluiceway that was capped in part because of the odor. That cap later was removed because of children drowning there, their lives immortalized with crosses near the river.

Today, beautification efforts reign.

An old Penn Central railroad trestle near Onondaga.

Near Rives Junction.

EATON RAPIDS

Called "Island City" because it is surrounded by the Grand and its Spring Brook tributary, Eaton Rapids is a Lansing bedroom community of about 5,000. Its distinctive features include Island Park as well as a number of current and former dam sites that inspire the annual Dam Festival.

Above: Locals Rebecca Finch and Lydia Pavalock walk along the edge of Island Park in Eaton Rapids.

Right: Pedestrian bridge to Howe Park.

Far right: Edgewater Apartments, with a porch that rivals the size of the Grand Hotel, casts a glow.

Grand River Expedition member Donovan Harper, of Alaska, flipped his wooden kayak and went under in a patch of whitewater while attempting to land his boat near the former Dimondale dam. Harper, who was uninjured, was thrown a rope and escorted by an aid boat.

THE MIDDLE GRAND

The middle part of the Grand River is all about power, and even a little awe.

Industrialists used the waterway to help power a business boom that eventually helped define Lansing. The river starts to gain significant strength in this stretch. Dams abound to harness that natural energy.

Upstream of Lansing in Grand Ledge, soaring rock formations stand sentry over the waterway, inviting climbers to test their mettle on the cliffs.

After Lyons, the Grand's final surge to Lake Michigan begins.

The crumbling Lyons Dam is little more than a speed bump on the Grand River. At just 9 feet high, it no longer holds back the water or powers grain mills.

Built in 1857 to drive industrial growth in this Ionia County village, however, the dam is symbolically huge.

River advocates believe an effort to remove the dam reflects a shift in the values that communities in the heart of the Grand River – from Lansing to Lyons – place on a waterway that fueled bountiful growth.

Those communities, which harnessed the Grand with dams and polluted its waters over the past two centuries, now view it as a valuable natural resource that still can drive healthy economic growth, environmental expert Dave Dempsey said.

"Historically, there has been a close but varying relationship of Lansing to the river," Dempsey said. "The river's potential for mill power is one of the reasons the city was founded; then, the river became a convenient sewer for individuals and industry."

Dempsey, an author and environmental adviser to former Gov. James Blanchard, said government-mandated pollution reductions and projects such as the 13-mile Lansing River Trail have changed the way people perceive and treat the Grand.

"There are still problems, but the attitude and practice toward the river is 100 percent better than a few decades ago," he said.

The fact that people now fish and paddle the winding stretch of the Grand that flows through Michigan's capital city is a small miracle, given the river's tortured past.

James MacLean, a historian at the Capital Area District Library, said newspaper ads for blocks of ice in the early 1900s, before the advent of refrigerators, were indicative of the river's putrid condition.

"There were ads that told people to buy 'upriver ice' – from upstream of Lansing – because the river water was cleaner there," MacLean said.

Downstream, the village of Lyons, population 742, marks the divide between the upper and lower Grand River watershed. The river gains most of its strength downstream of Lyons, where several major tributaries flow in: the Maple, Flat, Thornapple and Rogue.

In Lansing, however, the Grand first flexes its hydrologic muscle.

Nourished by the Red Cedar River, the flow picks up speed and – in its natural condition – created small rapids in several areas of town.

The steepest stretches of the river in the capital city now lie under dams and their reservoirs.

But from its wilderness days in the 1840s, the size and speed of the river helped Lansing to become an industrial powerhouse in the early 1900s, MacLean said.

"Lansing wouldn't be here without the river," he said, and would not even have been a settlement without the dam built by early arrivals to power sawmills and grain mills.

The Legislature's decision in 1847 to move the Capitol from Detroit to a more central location transformed the nondescript community into a regional center for commerce and manufacturing, according to Justin L. Kestenbaum's book, "Out of a Wilderness."

Forty years later, for example, R.E. Olds unveiled the first steam-driven horseless carriage, a contribution to the development of modern auto industry and, of course, the late Oldsmobile line.

By the early 1900s, the Grand at Lansing was lined not only with automakers but with lumber yards and carriage makers, flour mills, stone works, a brewery and cigar makers – all using river water for manufacturing processes – or waste disposal.

At the auto industry's peak in the early 1990s, Lansing laid claim to producing more vehicles than any other U.S. city.

Today, the city is in a period of industrial decline but urban renewal.

Though the industrial base is shrinking, downtown has blossomed with the Lansing River Trail, development of the $182 million State Accident Fund building and construction of the Michigan State Police headquarters – all along the Grand.

Despite progress in cleaning up the river in recent years, significant challenges remain.

The capital city holds the dubious honor of being the largest source of sewage overflows, according to state data. It dumped 694 million gallons into the Grand in 2008, up from 420 million in 2004.

By comparison, the city of Grand Rapids reduced overflows from 196 million gallons in 2004 to 11 million in 2008.

Lansing is in the midst of a 30-year, $500 million project to separate combined sewers that become overwhelmed during rain showers.

In Lyons, about 40 miles downstream, state officials believe similar increases in recreational activities will emerge once the village's antique dam – one of 232 on the Grand or its tributaries – is removed.

Lyons officials are trying to secure funding for the project, which could cost $1 million or more.

The cost may be staggering, but the environmental and economic benefits could be dramatic, said Scott Hanshue, a fishery research biologist for the Michigan Department of Natural Resources and Environment.

"I would expect recreational use of the river to increase as a result of the dam removal," Hanshue said. "Removing the dam will also restore some high gradient habitat utilized by many species of fish, so recreational fishing should also improve."

Lyons Village President Bernie Russell, who has lived in the community for 65 years, is one of the few village officials who want the dam restored.

"The dam has created a lot of memories," Russell said.

LANSING

Here the Grand first shows its busy side. Motorboats abound amid the tall buildings and riverfront improvements of the capital city.

Above: Boaters gather to listen to the offerings from the city's Common Ground Music Festival.

Right: A sunset serenade.

A beautiful day to be on the water. Int. 496 is the backdrop.

Lansing from above, with Cooley Law School Stadium, home of the Lansing Lugnuts minor league baseball team, featured prominently.

41

This page: The marled colors of dusk in Lansing.

Far right: Kevin Williamson paddles through downtown.

GRAND LEDGE

The ledges invite climbing even if there are two schools of thought in Grand Ledge: Let them climb, or preserve the ledges. Either way, the soaring rocky walls provide a dramatic backdrop to the Grand River, and leave no doubt the town is aptly named.

Left: The view downstream of Grand Ledge.

Right: Carl Sobel of Walker scales a grand ledge.

SHOCK THERAPY

Surveying the Grand from river-level is just scratching the surface.

Much of the true read of the waterway's health is below, and these underwater inhabitants are not inclined to spend much time in fresh air unless forced.

That is where fish shocking comes in.

In July, a Department of Natural Resources and Environment crew surveyed a two-mile stretch of river near the Portland State Game Area.

Experts used two boats. One contained booms and submersible electrodes that deliver a 200-volt, 6-amp current beneath the water to attract fish and temporarily stun them. A chase boat picked up the fish with soft nets; the fish then were put into holding tanks for data gathering before being released to the river a short time later.

Scott Hanshue, a DNRE fisheries management biologist, said the last such research was five years ago. Hanshue's team counted the species, measured their length and, for the game fish, snipped a tiny piece of dorsal fin to test growth rates.

"Growth rates tell us how well the fish community is doing," he said.

"All the species we saw are very sensitive to pollution. This stretch of the river is clean and has some of the nicest parts on the river."

Right: A small piece of dorsal fin from a small-mouthed bass is snipped and calculated to gather age information.

Opposite page: A greater Redhorse sucker is tossed in the holding tank.

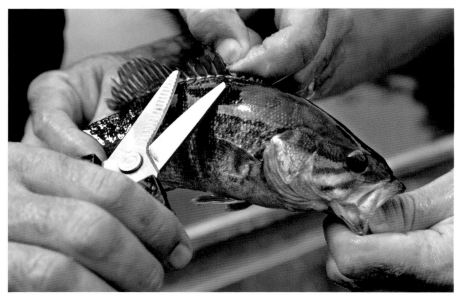

46

Monica Day and Larry Luce paddle out of Portland.

A little help from a sail.

Paddling along the Portland Municipal Dam.

PORTLAND

The Looking Glass meets the Grand in this "City of Two Rivers."
Settlers favored that intersection for trading post deliveries and
transportation. Today, city leaders have used the river as a focal
point of revitalization.

Above: A head start - portaging around the Portland Municipal Dam.
Right: Portland.

THE LOWER GRAND

The Grand River as it cuts through the Grand Valley is so familiar to us, yet it still holds some surprises.

Even as the Grand winds through the Grand Rapids metropolitan area, the sense from river level is often peaceful and remote, belying the development and bustling communities just beyond the banks. Birds you would only expect in the quieter upper reaches – like bald eagles and blue herons – soar overhead here, too.

Still, this is also where the Grand finally shows off the full effect of its might. Fully nourished by tributaries that are also the lifeblood of some of our suburban communities, the waterway is wide, the current swift.

We love to play in these waters, whether wading in near the fish ladder in Grand Rapids to try our luck during the salmon run or opening the throttle in Ottawa County.

For a river of contrasts, it's somehow fitting that while its final stretch is full of motorboats, they are hushed by no-wake rules in the Grand Haven channel.

Seems a respectful way for the Grand to end its journey into Lake Michigan.

From Lyons to Grand Haven, with the exception of the Fourth Street dam in Grand Rapids, the lower Grand River is open for passage.

It was once the unobstructed province of Indians and French fur traders and, later, steamships.

Today, the watery thoroughfare meanders through a changed landscape. The savannas and forests that once lined its banks have been replaced by modern features – a checkerboard of commerce, agriculture, homes, parks and playgrounds.

Scientists and others who study the river say the Grand is a mixed bag of good and bad. Naturally beautiful, scenic in many places, but communities along its length struggle with the byproducts of development.

Andy Bowman, planning director for the Grand Valley Metro Council and staff coordinator for the Lower Grand Organization of Watersheds program, said the lower river is better than it was. Progress has been made controlling pollution, but sedimentation and E. coli remain serious problems.

The E. coli comes from farm runoff and expanding suburbs and parks where a new dimension to the problem has developed.

"All the places where ducks get fed and Canada geese gather, places like Riverside Park and others along the river. They are all contributors," Bowman said. "That all goes directly into the river."

Grand Rapids, like other communities regulated by federal water quality laws, spent millions to separate its sanitary and storm sewer systems. The storm water isn't treated before being discharged to the river.

But where development occurs, where pavement and roof shingles substitute for percolating soils, an increasing volume of water flows into the storm system, bringing with it whatever residues lay on its surface.

Suburban septic systems also leach E. coli to ground and surface waters. It's a known problem, Bowman said, but diffuse and difficult to quantify. Point-source pollution (from discharge pipes) is now better controlled, but non-point source pollution is a growing problem.

This stretch shows the Grand's many faces. Its rich cultural heritage is not likely to be missed. Indian villages once dotted the river. Most inhabitants traveled by canoe. The French fur traders initially did likewise and later introduced European boat building technology in the form of the wooden "bateau," a flat-bottomed cargo hauler.

Commerce grew up along the river. "The Grand River was the highway," said Kevin Finney, executive director of the Great Lakes Lifeways Institute in Hopkins, a nonprofit educational organization focused on West Michigan's cultural heritage. "It wasn't until the mid-1830s and '40s that the trail and road system developed. The river was how you got around.

"Imagine downtown Grand Rapids as a big native settlement with a mile of cornfield on one side. Out in front were big, giant rapids. During the sturgeon run, the settlers said it looked like people could walk across the river on their backs. People who came here were floored by the immense beauty of the area."

The river at Saranac once offered Lamont button manufacturers raw materials. The pearly parts of native Grand River mussels were used to create buttons for dresses and other garments.

Today many of those mussels are endangered or gone. The button industry was closed down due to overharvest in the 1940s. Limited oversight of modern development proves to be the culprit today. Eroded sand and soils from home sites and buildings constructed along Grand River tributaries now regularly wash down into the Grand and quietly settle on top of native mussel beds, covering them.

Meanwhile upstream, closer to Ionia, the Grand is an important sanctuary for bald eagles. Scott Hanshue, the Michigan Department of Natural Resources and Environment fish habitat manager for the Grand River, called the area "critical over-winter habitat." More than 20 bald eagles can be seen there then.

The Flat River, well known for its spectacular smallmouth fishing, empties into the Grand here. It is a state-designated "Natural River," a special designation for unusual beauty and natural qualities that restricts certain types of development.

Fishing on the Grand, by contrast, could be a lot better, according to Hanshue. Its "degraded water quality" inhibits the productivity and diversity of fish species found there.

The river, he said, has more carp and rough fish than desired as a result. The dam at Fourth Street also plays an important role. It keeps various species from migrating upstream into waters they once inhabited.

The sturgeon is one example – it once was common upstream as far as Lyons. Great Lakes muskellunge, Michigan's biggest predator fish, is another.

Meanwhile the push to develop greenways along the river is reason for optimism, according to Hanshue.

The city of Grand Rapids instituted a planning process in 2002 which among other things calls for adding parks along the rivers and the expansion of green corridors and boosting river recreation.

In Ottawa County, parks director John Scholtz considers the natural areas and parks to be green gems. His agency began buying up riverside parcels in the 1990s, looking to establish a chain of green links along the river. His department currently manages 1,800 acres along the Grand in Ottawa County.

"We decided to focus on the river corridor greenway and the Lake Michigan coastline," Scholtz said. "We figured having connected habitat is more desirable than a park that is an island of green space."

Crockery Creek Natural Area is a prime example. The 331-acre parcel in Crockery Township protects a half mile of Grand River frontage and a couple of miles of Crockery creek, a tributary to the Grand. It is one of the wilder areas within the park system, Scholtz said.

"There is an active eagle nest there and the creek is big enough for canoes and kayaks," Scholtz said. "It is scenic, wild and has unusual plants. You feel like you are discovering something when you go there."

WEBBER DAM

The dam in Ionia County, south of Lyons, is one of 13 hydroelectric dams operated by Consumers Energy. It started operating in 1907 and is the tallest dam on the Grand River.

Their own piece of peace: Donna Smit, owner of Riverbend Primitive Campground in Saranac, enjoys the river with other longtime campers.

Sunrise over Saranac.

Her own bubble machine: Theresa Eickholt of Grand Rapids has some fun during the expedition.

A winding slice of blue through an undeveloped section of land.

PROJECT LAKEWELL

Centuries ago, the Grand was a vital life source for people, providing the necessary means for transportation for everyone from Indians to fur traders.

Project Lakewell brought that history to life.

Group members, carrying a message of protecting and preserving the water and wildlife, paddled part of the expedition while wearing garb from the 1700s that depicted some of the people who may have used the river in that era.

continued on page 65

One such character, portrayed by Project Lakewell director Lynn Johnson, was "Bear Woman, a wealthy fur trader, half Ojibwa, half French."

Johnson sees more in the Grand than meets the eye.

"This is sacred water. We used to drink it, and it was a highway that brought people together."

Far left: Project Lakewell director Lynn Johnson wears the traditional 18th century clothing of the Ojibwa.

Left: Ray Drysdale of Albion portrays Sinnanatha ("Big Fish"), a fur trader from the 1700s.

RIVER LIVING

Sure, the Grand floods homes here. Call it a test of tolerance that is ultimately a labor of love for those who endure.

Some residents cannot abide the high waters and leave. But for those who muddle through the wet times, they say they receive the ultimate reward: their own piece of wilderness in the city's backyard.

Their retreat is just outside the door, where like-minded residents take in the quiet, hop in their pontoons for a cruise full of neighborly greetings and live every day the life some people travel hours to experience for just a moment in time.

Above and right: Buzz and Peggy Trudell have lived on the Grand River for more than a quarter century.

Far right: Housesitting with a view: Heather Brusnahan dangles her feet in the water of a backyard of a friend's house, where she kept watch for a time.

High water mark: Kevin Walker of Plainfield Township stands under a sign denoting the water line from a flood in 1904.

Tyler Clifford swings from a rope in his backyard.

A boat motor converted to a mailbox.

Far left: Cousins Stephen White and Parker Wallace build a fire in the backyard of their grandparents' home.

Left: Horace Anderson of Belmont stands beside an old swing, worn from many grandchildren, in the backyard of the home where he has lived for 27 years.

Gilbert Olds stretches out in his perfectly situated lounge chair.

Gretchen Dietrich waves to a neighbor from her pontoon boat on the Grand River. Grandson Stephen White of Howard City sits behind her.

Right: Douglas Jackson, who has lived on the Grand since 1963, participates in a walleye contest with his neighbors each summer.

Far right: Molly Grant plays with her yellow lab, Sadie, at her family's campsite near Lowell.

GRAND RAPIDS

The state's second-largest city owes its name fully to the Grand River. Indeed, Grand Rapids once had powerful rapids. Those were tamed by damming in the 1800s, but the river here still has a swift current that is not fully appreciated until one is next to it – or in it. With its network of bridges and overpasses, it seems the most common activity near the river in Grand Rapids is crossing it, but increasingly residents, visitors and community leaders are appreciating the special features the Grand has to offer.

The view from under the Blue Bridge between Fulton and Pearl streets.

Grand Rapids from above, day and night.

A foggy dawn's first light: Anglers are out early under the Bridge Street bridge to try their luck against a backdrop of lights that aren't quite ready to let go of the night.

Their own public island.

Quick current, more fish: Braving the swift waters near the Fourth Street Dam for the best steelhead catch.

Above: First shot of the 2010 Fourth of July fireworks.

Right: Slicing through the Grand during a regatta.

Far right: A seagull does some aerial fishing near a downtown coffer dam.

GRAND LADY

Its dock near the Wilson Avenue bridge is visible from busy Int. 196, but riding on the 150-passenger paddle wheeler gives little hint of the populated township – Georgetown – it first travels through. With birds of prey overhead and houses or other signs of life minimal, owner Bill Boynton imagines the river doesn't look much different in this stretch than it did centuries ago.

Opposite page: Boynton steers the 40-foot vessel he built.

GET YOUR MOTOR RUNNING

Seems only right they are called pleasure craft.

On a warm sunny day, the Grand is a conduit for speed boats pulling out of huge marinas in Grand Haven headed for the ultimate boating playground: Lake Michigan.

But don't discount what the Grand offers to those looking to motor about.

There's nothing more relaxing than a pontoon trip along the waterway, taking in the sights of other boaters and hidden pockets of nature and peace. Or think how much a fishing trip is enhanced with the help of a trolling motor.

As this is the Grand River, though, it's not all about a quiet little cruise. If you want to open up the throttle, there are spots where you can.

Once it's time to end the fun, not only do the big marinas await, but also quaint little ones upstream, some reminding us of a different time. After all, generations have loved this river.

Opposite page: Under repair – Richard Burnett's twin outboard boat is pulled from the river for repairs at Southern Grand Marina.

The Grand Isle Marina in Grand Haven.

FELIX

The network of bayous around the Grand River in western Ottawa County has a bit of a personal feel, with singular names like Lloyd and Bruce.

On one of these bayous – Stearns, to be exact – you'll find another singular name: Felix's.

Felix Pytlinski, 79, has a little shop and marina on the river in Robinson Township. His father opened the place on the Fourth of July in 1929.

Pytlinski eventually took over the business from his father, and got out of outboard motor and boat sales in the 1980s, but still docks a few pontoons and small fishing boats. He said Grand River Expedition co-founder and paddling legend Verlen Kruger bought a kayak from the shop in the 1960s.

These days, Pytlinski specializes in old gun and collectible knife sales.

Ashleigh Tallman sits on a pontoon docked at the closed Grand Valley Marina in Crockery Township.

Fishing at the Grand River channel under the U.S. 31 drawbridge.

Heading under the drawbridge.

A motor yacht cruises past an old railroad bridge and piles of stone aggregate at Verplank Dock Company in Ferrysburg.

The river ends at Lake Michigan.

Almost there: The river becomes a delta just before Lake Michigan.

THE EXPEDITION

They endured pouring rain and searing heat, waters so slow that they earned every stroke, and waters so fast that they had to become one with adrenaline. And so often, they found peace and beauty, sometimes in unexpected places. These expedition paddlers rode out every change the river threw at them, and came away with a better appreciation of each other and of the waterway they called home for much of July 2010.

When I drive over the Grand River these days, I think differently about it than I once did. The water downtown is no less brown when it rains. The drab concrete seawalls remain in place. And yet, somehow, the river seems a friendlier place.

I confess that in the days following the 2010 Grand River Expedition, I occasionally stole away during lunch breaks to sit by the river as though it was an ailing old friend, but one no longer in critical condition, one whose recovery could be viewed with optimism and hope.

These days I look at the river with anticipation rather than indifference. Where might I take the kayak with friends? Which stretch will yield the sight of a bald eagle? How old will I be when the next expedition paddles its length in 2020?

The Grand was once a place I avoided like the plague. One does not play in a sanitary sewer. One doesn't relax when body contact may mean contracting a disease.

For years I'd fish it now and then for a story, but there seemed little reason to go otherwise given the plethora of clean water options elsewhere.

That stigma, unfortunately, still remains, though it is dwindling. Buried in my desk somewhere is a small brown foam fly sent in by a reader following a story I wrote about fishing the Grand. "Mr. Meyerson," he wrote, "here is a fly I tied for fishing the Grand River. I call it the Fecal Dun Deluxe, otherwise known as the Doo-doo Bug."

It was a funny, but sad commentary about the water quality in the Grand, Michigan's longest river, the very one that runs through the heart of many communities like Grand Rapids, Lansing and Jackson. But that was also a time when raw sewage overflows often contaminated the river, when "floaters" meant something other than surface flies.

My change of heart isn't the result of wishful thinking. Having spent nearly two months researching the river's history and character and another eight days paddling 150 miles of it, I had a chance to see a good deal of it and experience it intimately. I was never inclined to lick my fingers, but I did come to appreciate the progress that has been made cleaning up the river.

The Grand is beautiful in many places. It is wild feeling in others. There are segments where nature is alive and well, where a day on the river feels remote. All of that came as a surprise to me.

One of my favorite segments was just downstream from Rives Junction. It was a peaceful float through mature forest lands where birds were flying, where the sunlight filtered through the trees and there was just enough clearance around downed trees to keep it feeling wild.

It is wild feeling in others.

Another special place was upstream from Dimondale, in Ingham County, where several adjoining properties, the McNamara Canoe Landing, Riverbend Natural Area and Burchfield Park create a delightful greenway along the river. It was both accessible and inviting. Steps constructed at intervals downstream gave hikers access to the river and invited paddlers to come stretch their legs.

Paddling through Jackson's former sanitary sewer proved a hoot. It's been beautified. But upstream, in the slower seemingly forgotten slough that is also the Grand, the paddling was murky and uninspiring – like canoeing through an industrial park ditch.

Near Ada there was one day that I quietly cursed an inattentive farmer who allowed cattle to wander into the river and relieve themselves. The well worn path up the bank to the pasture said it wasn't the first time.

Grand Rapids Mayor George Heartwell had it right when he said: "Our understanding about the river has shifted dramatically in the last decade or two. It has shifted away from being a toilet, a place to wash away our industrial sins and sewage spills."

Right, but with further progress needed. Obviously, not everyone gets it.

Downstream of Grand Rapids, the river eventually widens and loses its intimate qualities, but there are miles of beautiful water that could and should be enjoyed by paddlers, boaters and

anglers without worry. Yet agricultural and livestock runoff are a problem.

The river, Heartwell said, is becoming "a gathering place where people can come together for conversation on its banks or to walk or watch people fish or kayak."

We can only hope so. It was that way three centuries ago when Indian villages dotted the Grand River corridor. Much of the river remained in a natural state and the communities that lived beside it stressed living in harmony with the land and water.

These are different times, to be sure, but that goal is no less worthy today.

Howard Meyerson, who wrote these reflections about his time on the expedition, paddles.

A kayak tiki God for good luck.

Getting ready to shove off on the first day.

A little help: Righting the kayaks to launch.

Kayak over troubled water: DNRE Sgt. Troy Bahlau helps Linda McMillan over the first challenging spot, near Michigan Center.

On a break in Jackson

Erich Ditschman and his son Jake, of East Lansing, paddle through Jackson. Ditschman, who did dialysis during the expedition, raised funds for the National Kidney Foundation during this trip.

109

David Ringlein and daughter Liz, of Lansing, launch at Rives Junction.

Pat Raimer of Lowell has a good laugh.

Above: Nature's obstacle course near Tompkins.

Right: The river starts to widen as paddlers cruise through Birchfield Park near Holt.

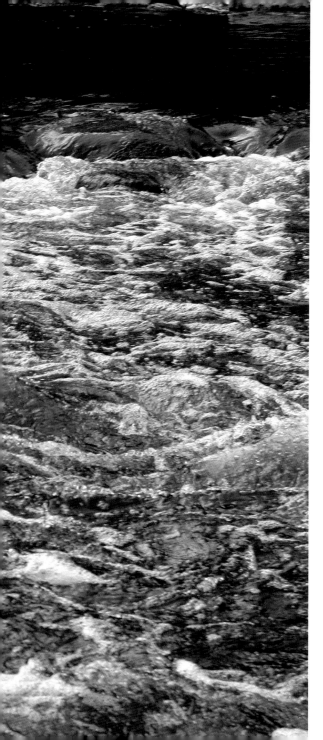

Feeling great: Gloria Miller smiles as she paddles between Michigan Center and Jackson. She would celebrate her 85th birthday later in the expedition.

A paddler benefits from the whitewater created when officials removed a dam near Dimondale, done in part to make the river more recreational.

Tim Williams of Saranac and his family joined the expedition for a day when it went through their community.

Christian Miller of Grand Haven rests during a lunch break in Lansing.

Paying tribute: Paddlers gather around a statue in Portland of legendary paddler and expedition co-founder Verlen Kruger.

Project Lakewell boat between Ada and Grand Rapids.

Diane Ward cools off in the Grand.

Zig zag: Ada is visible at the top of the picture.

There's room for everyone: The expedition heads into downtown Grand Rapids.

Liutauras Gedvilas takes in downtown from river level.

A bird's eye view of the expedition.

Paddlers pass under the U.S. 31 drawbridge in Grand Haven in their final leg of the expedition.

Complete with a Coast Guard escort, the paddlers finish their journey.

Diane Ward and John McCubbin congratulate each other at Grand Haven's Chinook Pier after finishing their two-week journey.

Donovan Harper puts his game face on.

Photography Index

All photos available for purchase. Contact The Grand Rapids Press at 616-222-5400.

THE GRAND RIVER

GRAND RIVER BY THE NUMBERS

5,572: Square miles in the Grand River watershed, or drainage basin.

2: Rank of Grand River watershed's size among all Michigan river systems. Only the Saginaw River drains more land.

13: Percentage of the Lake Michigan watershed that falls within the boundaries of the Grand River watershed.

53: Percentage of land in the Grand River watershed used for agriculture.

19: Counties that drain into the Grand River.

552: Descent of the Grand, in feet, between the headwaters, near Jackson, and the river mouth in Grand Haven.

232: Dams in the Grand River and its tributaries.

14: Dams in the river.

27: Percentage of land in the watershed considered urban.

20: Percentage of land in the watershed that is forest.

108: Fish species that inhabit the Grand River watershed.

95: Native fish species in the watershed.

13: Invasive fish species.

218: Species of birds that inhabit the watershed.

4 billion: Average daily flow of the river, in gallons, at Grand Rapids during 2009 (The equivalent of 6,067 Olympic-sized swimming pools).